THE

EPISTLE OF JAMES,

PRACTICALLY EXPLAINED,

BY

DR. AUGUSTUS NEANDER.

TRANSLATED FROM THE GERMAN

BY

MRS. H. C. CONANT.

"Why call ye me Lord, Lord, and do not the things which I say?"

WIPF & STOCK · Eugene, Oregon

Wipf and Stock Publishers
199 W 8th Ave, Suite 3
Eugene, OR 97401

The Epistle of James, Practically Explained
By Neander, Augustus
ISBN 13: 978-1-60608-683-4
Publication date 8/21/2009
Previously published by Sheldon & Co., 1858

It is with great pleasure that the translator offers to the Christian public, the second number of Neander's Practical Expositions, believing that it will be found no less interesting than the preceding volume on the Epistle to the Philippians. It is characterized by the same masterly power of development, the same depth and fulness of Christian experience. Seed-thoughts crowd every page; and many single passages, in sublimity of moral sentiment and beauty of illustration, equal anything which Neander has written. As being more strictly practical in its character, and elucidating a portion of the Divine word less understood, it may be even more generally acceptable and useful than the former Exposition. It restores to us, so to speak, one of the lost treasures of the church; for no part of the New Testament has been more misunderstood and perverted, or suffered more general neglect, than this Epistle. Luther rejected it without ceremony, calling it "an epistle of straw;" and many more timid minds have been greatly perplexed by its apparent contrariety to the doctrines of grace. The discussion of its character and claims, hitherto confined to scholars, is here presented in a form intelligible and practically useful to common Christians.

By the light of Neander's comprehensive mind, we see in James not the opponent of Paul, or of the great doctrine of justification by faith alone; but the earnest expounder of that "Law of Liberty," of which justification by faith is the chief corner-stone. Paul develops the principle; James depicts its results in the life. Paul unfolds the great love of God towards us; James points out the tests, whether this love has been received into our hearts and become there the vitalizing, reigning principle. It is the tree known by its fruit, the enkindled light by the light which it imparts, the life within by the outward signs of life. In the personality of James, and the character of the churches whom he addressed, we find the true key to this Epistle. Placed side by side with the Sermon on the Mount, it is seen to be a faithful reflection of that divine original; its whole essence and intent being comprised in those words of our Saviour, which we have prefixed to this volume as its most appropriate motto: "Why call ye me Lord, Lord, and do not the things which I say!"

One opinion advanced in the author's introductory remarks, viz., that James was not an Apostle, may not gain the assent of all his readers. Neander himself formerly held,[*] with many other distinguished critics, that this epistle was written by the Apostle James, the son of Alpheus and of Mary the sister of our Lord's mother; who, as being the near kinsman of the Lord, was in accordance with Jewish usage called his brother. The writer may be permitted to suggest that the practical inferences, here so skilfully traced, might be drawn, though not indeed with equal force, from the author's earlier view. James, as the Lord's own brother, or as a near kinsman, must in either case have been subject to very similar influences, arising from near earthly relationship to Christ. In the exposition itself, there is nothing at variance with

[*] Paulus und Jacobus, 1822.

either supposition. Nor does either view affect what Neander so truthfully says of the relations of the mother of Jesus, and of the contrast between the earthly and the spiritual; since there were, as we have every reason to believe, "brothers of the Lord" in the strictest sense.

To facilitate the use of the translation, the first part has been divided into sections with a brief statement of the contents of each, for which the translator is responsible. The quotations from the Epistle are given in the words of the English version, with the author's variations in brackets wherever they are made the basis of his view.

The third and last number of this series, the Exposition of the First Epistle of John, was prepared for the press by the author, and has been given to the public since his decease. A translation of it will follow as soon as practicable.

H. C. C.

ROCHESTER, N. Y., Jan. 1852.

THE EPISTLE OF JAMES.

INTRODUCTION.

§ 1. *Diversities in modes of religious development, and in the consequent forms of faith.*

It is the remark of one of the early Church Fathers, that what Paul says of himself,—viz. that he became all things to all men, that he might win all to the Gospel,—is true in a still higher degree of Him who was in this the Apostle's pattern, of Christ himself. We see it in that manifold variety of manner, adapted to all the varieties in human character and relations, by which, both in his personal labors on earth, and in his spiritual revelations among all nations since his ascension, he has drawn men to a saving knowledge of himself. His manner, while laboring upon earth, is indeed an image of that invisible divine agency extending through all times, in which he evermore reveals himself as the same yesterday, to-day, and forever. This diversity Christ himself indicates, in those parables in which he describes how the kingdom of God is found; showing at the same time the one thing, in which all must finally agree who would become partakers of the kingdom of God, and the varieties of way and manner in which they are conducted thither. Only those attain to the kingdom of God who enter it by violence. Only those find the treasure hidden in the field, who are ready to sell all they have that they may become possessors of that field. Only those secure possession of that precious pearl, outshining in beauty and splendor all beside, who prize it above all else, and shun no pains, no cost to win it for themselves,— esteeming all other good as nothing, for the sake of that one highest good, the kingdom of God.

But in order to bring men to this decision of purpose, without which none can enter the kingdom of God, they must be acted on in various ways suited to their various characters and circumstances. Some are like the merchant, who having spared no pains or cost to find precious pearls, at length, through this earnest and laborious search, secures possession of that richest of all jewels. Such are those, who, impelled by longing after some satisfying good, already have sought it long in vain. They have found many things which satisfy in part; but in the end have learned, that of all these not one can give the spirit full and lasting satisfaction. Thus they are ever beginning the search anew, till at length, through this ever-renewed effort they attain to that one highest good, and find in it the full satisfaction which their souls require. Others again, seeking no treasure, come unawares upon the field containing it, and find it as it were by accident. Such are those, in whom the longing after the highest good, the kingdom of God, has not yet been awakened; who are surprised by an unsought gift, which imparts to their souls a satisfaction never imagined and never sought. The one class, by a gradual progressive development out of a life, in which preparative grace had from the first given tokens of its active presence, quickening and unfolding by various means the life-germ in the higher nature,—had thus been finally drawn into full fellowship with the Lord. The other, willing slaves of passions that long withstood the divine call, had been drawn at length, as by a power that constrained their resisting will, to him whose love seeks the deliverance of all.

Since now the mode of development is so different in the two cases, so also will be the form which faith assumes in each. To the one, the new state to which he has attained will seem but as the aim and completion of that earlier one, which by many progressive steps conducted to and ended in it; and that earlier form of life, out of which he passed into this new state, will always remain to him a dear and familiar one. To the view of the other, the new state will present itself as in direct opposition to the old. These two forms of conception are both founded in truth; each will, in its peculiar manner, contribute to the glory and furtherance of Christianity. The first is especially adapted to show, how all that preceded this new state was designed to prepare the way for it; and here the change will manifest itself in a less striking form. The second is certainly the more thorough and profound,—presenting a more complete development of the new life in its essential nature, in which it is exalted above all else.

This diversity and variety, observable in the whole process of development through which

Christianity has passed, in the entire history of the Church, appears also in the earliest stage of that process belonging to the apostolic age. But in its later history, we often find these differences,—which, as already indicated, should be mutually supplemental, serving each to complete the other,—separating the one from the other, and assuming the attitude of irreconcilable antagonism. The perception of the higher unity is wanting; although he who can recognize the One Christ in all his manifestations, partial as they may be and obscured by human narrowness of view, will be able even from this antagonism to deduce that higher unity. From this source have sprung those controversies, which have done so much to destroy rather than to edify. On the contrary, the relation of the great Teachers of the New Testament to one another, as exhibited to us in their lives and writings, enables us to view these manifold forms of conception as mutually completive; not excluding one another, but belonging together as parts of the same whole,—the One Christ in the broken rays of his manifold revelation through various organs.

It is in this light we are to regard James, the

brother of the Lord, as forming the counterpart to the great Apostle of the Gentiles. That we may be able rightly to understand and apply his Epistle, according to the plan adopted in our explanation of Paul's Epistle to the Philippians, we must first endeavor to form a distinct idea of his whole PERSONALITY, as exhibited in the circumstances of his personal development and in his labors, as well as in this Epistle.

§ 2. Personal relations and religious development of James.

In reference to the personality of James, the fact is an important one that he did not belong to the number of the Apostles. The Apostles were formed out of those disciples, who had attached themselves to the Redeemer with minds still undeveloped, and yielding with childlike susceptibility wholly to his influence. They had not been previously formed in another school, before coming into connection with him. Their whole development they had received in intercourse with him; and hence they were fitted, in a peculiar manner, to become vessels of his all-transforming grace, to receive in themselves a faithful impress of his image, and to serve as instruments for the diffusion of his word and his spirit through all ages. With Paul it was far otherwise. He had, indeed, this in common with the rest of the Apostles, viz. that he could bear testimony as an eye-witness to the Risen Christ, and had received an immediate, personal impression of him. But he had come to Christ, with a well-defined system formed in a wholly different school; and hence, in his case, the new man in Christ must present in its development the strongest possible contrast with his earlier character.

Unlike to both of these cases was that of James. He was a brother of the Lord according to the flesh. All those passages of the Gospels in which "brothers of the Lord" are mentioned, together with Matt. i. 25, are most naturally explained on the supposition, that after the birth of Jesus Mary bore still other sons. These were the "brothers of the Lord," of whom James was one. Inasmuch as marriage and the production of offspring, like everything belonging to our nature, was to be sanctified through Christ, there is nothing in such a supposition which is at all questionable, nothing derogatory to the dignity of the mother of Christ, or to his own. If anything offensive is found in it, it is owing solely to a mistaken veneration of Mary, and to that false ascetic tendency, whose views of the unholiness of the married state, and of the superiority of celibacy, are entirely at variance with the spirit of Christianity. On the contrary, it is only when thus seen in contrast with the usual course of nature, that the birth of Jesus, as effected by supernatural agency, appears in its true light and its true significance. Christ, as the miraculously begotten son of Mary, then appears in contrast with the offspring of Mary according to the laws of natural descent; the contrast between the natural and the supernatural (as Paul designates it, Gal. iv. 23 and 29), between him that is born after the spirit and him that is born after the flesh; the contrast which pervades the whole process of development in the kingdom of God.

James was therefore, in his religious development, distinguished from the other preachers of the Gospel, in that it neither proceeded so entirely and from its first beginnings from Christ himself as was the case with the other Apostles,—nor formed itself out of such a contrast between the earlier and the later, as appears in the case of Paul. His path of development, originating elsewhere, moved on for a time independently beside that circle of influences, which had formed itself from and around Christ, and not till a later period became wholly united with it.

Now it might seem, indeed, that one so closely connected with the Lord as his own brother, the daily witness of his life and actions, was the one fitted above all others to become his disciple; that one so pre-eminently favored from the first, must have been in many respects in advance of the Apostles themselves. On this view was founded the judgment of the common Jewish Christians, that they were bound to exalt James above all other preachers of the Gospel, and to pay special respect to his authority.

In the estimation thus formed of him, by the standard of the merely external natural relation to Christ, we perceive the intermingling of the Jewish spirit in the conception of Christianity,—its opposite constituting the true Christian standpoint; as, in general, the disposition to the outward and formal in religious things is Jewish, while the tendency to the inward and spiritual belongs to the nature of Christianity. The internal and external stand not seldom in inverse proportion to each other. He who stood in the nearest external relations to the revelation of the kingdom of God, to the manifestation of the divine in humanity, to the appearance of the Son of God,— might inwardly be farthest from it, and so remain if he stopped at the external manifestation, if he accustomed himself to see only with the bodily eye, and through this habit was hindered from penetrating with the eye of the spirit to that which was within. This we see in the whole relation of the Jews to the kingdom of God, and to the Messiah who proceeded from the midst of this people, destined to prepare the way for his manifestation. Christ himself testifies, in opposition to this outward Jewish tendency, that the external natural relation is of no account; that all depends rather on the inward relation, formed by the direction of the mind and heart; that not natural relationship, but submission of the soul, can alone bring one into union with him. So on one occasion, when he was occupied with his life-work, the preaching of the Gospel, among those who listened to his words with eager and receptive hearts; he repelled those who would interrupt him on the plea that his nearest kindred, his mother and brethren, desired to see him. Pointing to the circle of disciples, in whom the seed of the divine word was received into the good soil of receptive and retentive hearts, he said: "My mother and my brethren are THESE, who hear the word of God and do it." (Luke viii. 21, Mark iii. 34, 35.) Thus the essential point is not, how one is related to him by natural descent, but how he is in spirit related to the divine will revealed by him. Here also belongs the incident related Luke xi. 27, 28. A woman, powerfully affected by the divine impression of his words, cried out from the midst of the listening multitude: "Blessed is the womb that bare thee, and the breasts which thou hast sucked!" "Yea rather," he replied, implying the vanity of this supposed advantage, "blessed are they who hear the word of God and keep it!" Prophetic warnings! Not only against that externalizing tendency, as shown in the admixture of the old Jewish spirit with Christianity,—but against that same spirit as it has often, in later times and under other forms, reappeared in the Christian Church!

Thus the very thing, which might seem most favorable to the religious development of James, turned to his disadvantage. The saying which Christ used in reference to his fellow-townsmen among whom the greater part of his life had been spent, and who had been eye-witnesses of his progressive development from childhood,—"A prophet is of no honor in his own country,"—applies with equal force to the case of James and his brothers. For the very reason, that they had from the first been eye-witnesses of the human earthly development of the Son of Man, they were not able to penetrate beyond the outward human veil. It became to them a stone of stumbling. True they afterwards witnessed the revelation of the Son of God, both in the inward power of the divine life perceptible only to the inwardly awakened sense for the divine, and in those proofs of power exhibited in his miracles. Still the faith, thus at times awakened, gave way continually to that skepticism proceeding from the prejudices of the natural man, who judges only after the flesh and by the outward appearance; and thus, during the whole earthly life of Christ, they remained in this state of vacillation, wavering between faith and unbelief. But when that stone of stumbling was taken out of their way, and the Son of God no longer stood before their eyes in the earthly veil of the Son of Man; when He, who was believed dead, showed himself victorious over death and living in divine power, to those whose weak faith required such confirmation; it was then, that the decisive and final direction was given to the development of the religious life of James (1 Cor. xv. 7). From this time forward we see in him the decided, unwavering, zealous witness of the faith in that Jesus, as his Messiah, Lord and Saviour, who had been his own brother according to the flesh. (James i. 1.)

§ 3. Stand-point of James as an inspired teacher, and his relation to Paul.

The manner, however, in which he testified of Christ, took its character from his previous training and course of life. He, above all others, stood on the ground of Jewish piety in the Old Testament forms; and had already completely developed himself within this sphere, when he was led to that decisive faith in Jesus, as the Messiah promised in the Old Testament. From this new point of view, his previous Judaism unfolded itself in its true and full import. Christianity now appears to him as the true Judaism. The spirit which proceeds from Christ explains the forms of the Old Testament, and leads them to their proper fulfilment. The position of James is precisely that taken by Christ in the Sermon on the Mount; which contains the germ of all that is peculiar to the Gospel, without expressly declaring the abrogation of the Law; where all is presented under the idea of the kingdom of God, and the reference of each particular to the person of Christ, though everywhere implied and forming the central point of all, is nowhere asserted in words. Hence in the development of the divine kingdom,—where as in all the works of God, the works of grace as well as of nature, no chasms are allowed but all proceeds by progressive steps,—James forms a very important transition-point from the Old to the New Testament. Something would be wanting to us, if we had not James in the New Testament. And that narrowness of view, which disdains to follow patiently this gradual development,—demanding everywhere and at once the perfected form,—may find its punishment in the consequent incompleteness of its own Christian knowledge. As a means of leading pious Jews to faith in the Gospel, this position of James was of special use. Just in proportion as it would have been detrimental to a Paul, whose mission was the conversion of the heathen nations, was it advantageous to James in the sphere of labor assigned to him in Palestine, and particularly in Jerusalem among unmixed Jews. Thus divine wisdom manifests itself in assigning to each his sphere, his peculiar mission in the development of the kingdom of God, adapted to his peculiar qualifications. The sole concern is that each rightly fulfil his appointed mission, understand and faithfully adhere to his prescribed limits; while at the same time he recognizes the divine call in him also, to whom as the possessor of other gifts another sphere of labor has been assigned,—and is willing to regard their several spheres as each the complement of the other. Such was the relation of James to Paul.

James did indeed know, from the first, what the voice of prophecy had indicated, of the coming extension of Jehovah's worship among the heathen nations, and of their participation in the blessings of the divine kingdom,—a glory which belonged to Messianic times,—and also that this was to be fulfilled through Christ as the Messiah. But the possibility of a worship of Jehovah except in the old legal forms, or of a participation in the kingdom of God in any other way, remained hidden from him at first, even after he had attained to a settled faith in Jesus as the Messiah. The intimations in the discourses of Christ that his word should become the leaven, which, by an indwelling power alone and independently of all else, should penetrate the life of humanity; in Jews and Gentiles alike leavening all and forming it anew; that the new spirit of Christianity should burst asunder and break through the forms of legal Judaism; these intimations he did not yet understand. This belonged to those things of which Christ said, in his parting words to his disciples, that what they could not yet comprehend should afterwards be revealed to them by the Holy Spirit. But this revelation of the Holy Spirit was not imparted to all at the same time, nor in the same way. This too was determined by the different stand-points from which they had attained to faith in the Gospel. Accordingly, more or less of preparation might be required for leading them to that more perfect knowledge; it might be effected more by a process of thought inspired and guided by the Holy Spirit, and thus enabled to develop and apprehend the whole sum of revealed truth,—or it might be more the effect of immediate illumination by the Divine Spirit. In the history of the church, we meet with many melancholy examples of opposition and estrangement, when the spiritual insight attained by one is still withheld from another, and the one thus becomes free from the narrow limits in which the other is still confined. Even in the apostolic church, this was the source of much disunion and division.

But James was far from that narrow obstinacy of temper, which would not allow any stand-point but his own; would permit no opposing facts to influence his convictions,—promptly rejecting the truth revealed to others because it was not imparted through him, and thus setting bounds to the farther development of the kingdom of God. When, at the apostolic conference (Acts xv.), the controverted point respecting the observance of the Mosaic law was for the first time discussed, and Peter and Paul bore testimony to the effects of the Gospel among believing Gentiles, who had not submitted to circumcision, nor in any other respect to the observance of the Law; these undeniable facts were proof enough for James, that through faith in the Saviour, the same divine results were produced among the heathen as among believing Jews. In this he saw a fulfilment of the Old Testament predictions; and he now learned their true aim and import, as he had never understood it before. The mild conciliating spirit of James is shown, by the manner in which he sought to reconcile the differences between the Jewish and Gentile Christians. He could do justice to a stand-point wholly different from his own. Believing Gentiles, on the ground of their faith merely, were to be admitted to equality with believing Jews in the fellowship of the divine kingdom; only, for the furtherance of harmony with believers from among the Jews, they were to conform in certain external points, which might also serve to withhold them from participation in everything connected with heathen worship. But while James recognized the equality of churches consisting of uncircumcised Gentiles, and allowed to the preaching of the Gospel among the Gentiles its own rights as an independent calling; he at the same time remained true to his own peculiar stand-point, according to which the old forms were to be continued as depositories of the new spirit, and the Jews were to retain their religious nationality unchanged. Still, as we see from the Acts of the Apostles, he was ever the mediator between Paul and the zealots among the Jewish Christians, who were prejudiced against him. Here too he always conducted in the same spirit of mildness and conciliation.

§ 4. Character and condition of the Churches to whom the Epistle was addressed, and nature of the errors against which it was directed.

In order now to understand and rightly apply the Epistle of James, we must endeavor to form a distinct conception of those to whom it was addressed, and whose peculiar circumstances he had especially in view.

We can, indeed, say nothing definite in regard to the region where these churches are to be sought. The Epistle itself furnishes only general information, sufficient, however, for the practical purposes we have now in view. The essential points are these: There were churches consisting exclusively of Christians of Jewish origin, in which all the practical errors of Judaism were associated with faith in Jesus as the Messiah; and in which there were many, who gave little or no evidence of the new creation which is the necessary product of that faith.

That wholly earthly direction of mind, which was often connected with false zeal for the honor of God; the insatiable love of gain, and consequent divisions from the clashing of selfish interests; these were the faults which they had brought with them from their earlier Jewish state, into their new Christian relation. The aristocracy of wealth held in check the pervading spirit of Christian love, whose office it is to repress and triumph over all earthly distinctions. Instead of being obliterated by that spirit of love, the distinctions caused by the unequal distribution of wealth, were recognized and maintained at the expense of that fraternal relation, which should characterize a community of Christians. Furthermore, it belonged to the defects of this false Jewish spirit, that, instead of regarding piety as a whole, proceeding from the inward temper of the heart and embracing the entire life; it held only to particular observances of the outward life, in which piety should manifest itself,—that tendency to the external in religion of which we have spoken. This manifested itself in the great value attached to external descent from the theocratic people, to circumcision and the works of the Law, making justification dependent thereon. This same spirit now passed over to the Jewish Christians; and became especially prominent, wherever they had the ascendency in opposition to Gentiles and Gentile Christians.

This tendency was one which, from its very nature, belongs exclusively to no age; it was no mere thing of the past, extinguished with Judaism once for all, and never to reappear in the Christian church. The declaration of the preacher of wisdom is applicable here,—that "what has been will be, and there is nothing new under the sun." What we here term the Jewish spirit, had not its origin in anything inherent in Judaism as a divine institution; but is to be referred rather to the nature of the unrenewed man, drawing down the divine to his own level, and seeking to appropriate it to himself without renouncing his own peculiar nature. Now as the nature of the unrenewed man remains ever the same, there must at all times proceed from it this same erroneous tendency, which we may characterize as in its spirit and nature Jewish.

This Jewish spirit shows itself equally, when the unrenewed nature of man mingles its disturbing influence with the conception of Christianity. It is seen in the disposition to value one's self on the ground of descent from a Christian people, or from some particular nation distinguished in earlier times for its piety, and on this account assigned a more conspicuous place in the history of God's kingdom; without considering that if his own life does not correspond to the peculiar character and position of such a people, this connection, instead of being his glory, will become his condemnation. So is it also with pretensions based on a father's pious deeds, without any effort to imitate his example. So is it when connection with a particular church is made one's only boast, his sole ground of hope, and no importance is attached to the practice of genuine Christianity; when, in short, in the outward organization of the church, the essence of Christianity itself is forgotten. In each and all of these cases, we perceive the same practical error of the Jewish spirit. So if we base our confidence on a zealous devotion to the external observances of Christian worship, attendance upon divine service, the celebration of the sacraments, without going beyond the outward form; this is in spirit precisely the same, as that Jewish reliance upon circumcision and the works of the Law. The name alone is changed; the thing itself remains the same. Hence all the arguments and warnings against such a tendency, which we find in Paul's Epistles, may be applied with equal propriety to these same practical errors in every age of the church, although the particular forms of it with which he contended may exist no longer.

It does not appear indeed, in the Epistle of James, that he combats this tendency in precisely these forms, as is the case in Paul's writings. Yet is the root, the essential tendency, the same. He is obliged to instruct his readers in the nature of true religion,—wherein that form of religion, of which they made so much account, must therefore have been deficient. It is only a different form of development which is here treated of; the same radical tendency is too obvious to be mistaken. There were two leading forms of this tendency. One of these consisted in an undue estimation of outward works of the Law. The other exalted the mere knowledge of the Law, of the true God and of what pertains to his worship, into the principal thing; and on the ground of knowledge merely,—of the mere profession of belief, of faith simply as an act of the understanding,—claimed superiority over the Gentiles, although the course of life by no means corresponded to this knowledge and outward profession. Paul likewise combats, in the second chapter of the Epistle to the Romans, this false reliance on mere knowledge of the Law. Of the same character was that dead learning in the Scriptures, such as Christ condemned in the Pharisees, who thought that in them they had eternal life, and yet would not be directed by them to him who alone could bestow eternal life. The consequence was, that each one was anxious to gain currency for his own religious views, to set himself up as a teacher for others, without first taking care to mould his own character in conformity with divine truth. Hence arose the contests between these would-be teachers; another form of that bias to the external and the literal, but springing from the same root as those before described,—no less capable of co-existing with an ungodly life, and of serving as a support for it.

The question now arises,—does the false idea of

faith and the over-estimation of mere faith, which James opposes in this Epistle, belong also to this same radical tendency; or are we to regard it as something different, and derived from another source? Do we find here so clear a reference to the Pauline idea of faith, as to make the conclusion necessary, that the doctrine of justification by faith, as taught by Paul, had been misunderstood and misapplied in these churches? Some might have imagined, that they could glory in justification solely by faith in the Redeemer, while they continued to live in the practice of sin. Against such misunderstanding and perversion, Paul himself seeks to guard his doctrine, in many passages of the Epistle to the Romans. In later times,—when the doctrine which Paul made it his especial object to maintain in opposition to Judaism and judaizing teachers, had been re-established in its rights by Luther, in opposition to a Jewish spirit which had once more crept into the church; there then followed a new service of the letter, a new phase of this tendency to outward forms, and again the connection between faith and life was rent asunder. Much which James says of this tendency in his day, might be applied to this case with equal propriety.

This question, whether James is here contending against a misapprehension of the Pauline doctrine, or has no reference whatever to it,—is by no means necessarily connected with the question of the relation of Paul's teaching to that of James. James might have intended to oppose a misunderstanding of Paul's doctrine,—nay, even the doctrine itself, if he had first met with it in this erroneous form, without previous understanding with Paul in regard to his object; and yet a perfect harmony might be shown to exist between the two methods of exhibiting truth, each serving as the complement of the other. For it may easily happen, when one man has formed,—in accordance with his peculiar course of training, and the bearing of the counter-view which is before his mind,—his own peculiar mode of conceiving and stating a truth; that the very opposition made to it by another, conceiving the same truth from a different point of view, may show their essential agreement,—what was intended to counteract serving only to explain and complete. Thus a representation of Christian truths, even if called forth by opposition to the peculiarly Pauline form of doctrine, might have found place as a completing link, in that collection of writings containing the original pure revelation of Christian truth. Both these forms of conception and teaching might constitute parts of the same whole, as being mutually completive, in the one revelation of the Holy Spirit through different human organs inspired by him. Their relation to each other must therefore be especially considered hereafter.*

Now although it is possible that such a form of externalizing, as the one we have mentioned, might attach itself to the Pauline doctrine, and though, as we have seen, this was afterwards actually the case; the question still remains, whether we are justified in assuming this in regard to the particular churches brought to our knowledge in this Epistle. It was in churches like these, formed among Jews and exclusively of Jewish converts, that a perversion of the Pauline doctrine was most unlikely to arise; inasmuch as the Pauline standpoint was one with which they had nothing in common. The Pauline view of faith presupposes the strongly marked distinction between **Law and**

* Page 36.

Gospel, a doctrinal position opposed to legal righteousness, to the merit of one's own works. Opposition to the Jewish tendency to externals was the precise ground on which it planted itself; and where that tendency prevailed, a perverted form of this view could as little gain admission as the view itself.

But to resume our question: may not this particular error,—the false idea of faith and over-estimation of mere faith,—which James opposes, be also traced back to the same radical tendency? Let us only compare what precedes and what follows the discussion of this topic in the second chapter. It is preceded (chap. i.) by a rebuke of those who founded an imaginary claim on the mere hearing of the word, on the mere knowledge of it, without holding themselves bound to practise it; to which is added the rebuke of a mere fancied and seeming service of God. What now is this but that very same spirit of reliance on the external, which manifests itself in a mere adherence to certain articles of faith,—faith in the one true God, the Messiah,—and on this ground alone claims to be righteous, without recognizing the demands of this faith upon the life? As knowledge and practice are at war with each other, so are faith and life. A merely theoretical faith corresponds exactly to a merely theoretical knowledge. The same man, who satisfies himself with being able to discourse much of the law without obeying it, is also the one who makes a boast of his faith, without holding himself bound to the practice of that which faith requires. The same man who finds the essence of religion in certain external works, and claims to be a true worshipper of God merely on the ground of professing the true religion, is the one also who claims to be accounted righteous through a faith which produces no works. If we turn now to what follows (chap. iii.), we find that James is here rebuking those who were ever ready to exalt themselves into teachers of others; but who, by teaching what they did not practice, made themselves the more liable to condemnation. What then is this but that same radical tendency over again? And on what ground should we be justified in rending the intermediate passage from its connection, and making it refer to something else, the explanation of which must be sought elsewhere than in this one radical tendency?

It is true, that in the manner cf meeting these errors, which we will now further consider, James is distinguished in a peculiar way from Paul. It is the more practical man in contrast with the more systematic; the man to whose wholly Jewish development, faith in Christ was superadded as the crown and completion,—in contrast with him, whose faith in Christ took the form of direct opposition to his earlier Jewish views, as the centre of a wholly new creation. Hence with James, opposition to error takes more the form of single propositions and exhortations; with Paul it is a connected view, in which all proceeds from one central point. With James the reference to Christ appears only as one particular among others, a peculiarity especially objected to this Epistle, as if Christ were not to be found in it; while with Paul, on the contrary, the chief object is to exalt Christ, who is everywhere placed foremost, and is everywhere represented as the centre of the whole life, from whom all is derived, to whom all is referred. But yet, in these single propositions and admonitions of James, we are able to trace the higher unity lying at the basis; and can show that all have reference to Christ as the living centre, even though he is not expressly named. There may be a form of moral development, which receives its true light and its true significance through reference to Him as its centre and source, although he is not expressly recognized by name; and his name may be often on the lips, while yet the whole inward character has formed itself without reference to Him. In this light we must now endeavor to understand the controversial and admonitory passages of this Epistle.

The churches to whom it was addressed consisted of rich and poor; and undoubtedly the latter were the more numerous class among the Christians. We know that the Gospel everywhere, and especially among the Jews, found freer entrance with the poor and lowly than among the rich and powerful. Not that riches in themselves exclude from the kingdom of God, or necessarily form a hindrance to faith in the Gospel. When Christ says, that it is easier for a camel to go through a needle's eye, than for a rich man to enter into the kingdom of God, he means such as he who gave occasion to these words; those to whom,—though perhaps unconsciously,—the earthly is the highest good; whose treasure being on earth cannot, therefore, be in heaven; whose heart belongs to the earth where their treasure is, and is therefore far from that direction towards heaven, without which no one can ever share in its blessedness. Indeed he himself adds in the same connection, that although the salvation of a rich man is impossible with men, i. e. by mere human means, yet with God all is possible. He would say by this, that divine help is needful, in order that riches may not prove a hindrance to the attainment of the kingdom of God. This then is the import of the words; not that riches in themselves are a hindrance to this object, but that misdirection of the affections into which the rich man more than others is liable to fall. The rich should be awakened to a consciousness of this, and should be incited by a sense of the difficulties inherent in his case, to apply to God for the strength which he needs; that even while in possession of all earthly riches, he may still keep his treasure in heaven and his heart directed thither. In this Epistle itself we learn what is necessary to the rich for this purpose. Yet though riches are not, in themselves, a hindrance to participation in the kingdom of God, still it was often the case among the Jews, that the rich and mighty forgot in worldly enjoyments the higher wants of the inner man; lost the fixed consciousness of dependence on Him, whose power confers and disposes all; imagining that they possessed all things, they had no room left for the feeling of want and of the necessity of deliverance from it. Thus too in the Old Testament, the rich, the proud, and the ungodly are often ranked together as of one class.

But every external situation may become, according to one's temper of mind, either a help or a hindrance to salvation; and nothing can here injure or promote his interests independently of his own will. Thus may poverty also,—that physical want which depresses the spiritual nature, which prevents the inner man from awaking to self-consciousness, and to the feeling of his higher spiritual wants,—prove an obstacle to the attainment of the kingdom of God. Poverty, too, has its peculiar dangers, and this is not overlooked in this Epistle. In general, however, it was the poor and lowly, pining under the oppressions of the rich and powerful, and under the pressure of physical want, who most readily felt the need of deliverance from spiritual want, from inward poverty of soul. On this feeling of physical need, could more easily be engrafted that consciousness of the soul's necessities, through which they might be conducted to the Saviour. As in their case, there was nothing to deceive the soul into a seeming satisfaction of its wants, they could the more easily be drawn to that which furnished the true satisfaction for all its higher necessities. Moreover, the poor in this world could more readily than the rich attain to that poverty of spirit, to which, as Christ says, belongs the kingdom of Heaven. Thus the Gospel found, among the Jews, a readier reception from the poor than from the rich; and on this account, Christians were reproachfully called The Poor. We do not mean by this, that all these poor who received the Gospel, had been led to it by true poverty of spirit, and had thus been prepared to receive, as poor and needy, the true riches of the Gospel. Among them too was to be found the influence of that carnal mind which prevailed among the Jews,—begetting, not the true hope of the heavenward directed spirit, but rather the expectation of a recompense for bodily privations in the imagined carnal enjoyments of the kingdom of Christ. Now the faith of such, if we choose to call it by that name, had its source in the carnal mind of the natural man; and hence, the earlier form of this natural man was transferred with them out of Judaism into a professed Christianity,—where it was, as we shall see, opposed and rebuked by James.

As the poorer and lower class, the Christians had, as we have intimated, much to suffer from the persecution and oppression of the powerful and rich; partly on account of their religion, partly for the promotion of selfish interests, their religion serving as the pretext. The rich who called themselves Christians without being so in truth, were infected with the common vice of the rich among the Jews, and failed in the exercise of love and even justice towards their poorer brethren in the faith. Accordingly, we find in this Epistle words of consolation and encouragement for the oppressed and suffering, and of rebuke for the rich both within and without the church.

EXPOSITION

OF THE EPISTLE.

Its opening words are addressed to the Suffering,—exhorting them to steadfastness and submission. "My brethren, count it [Ch. 1. 2, 3 all joy when ye fall into divers temptations." The idea of temptation is a comprehensive one in the Scriptures. By it is designated, whatever may become an obstacle or impediment to Christian faith and Christian virtue,—prosperity and adversity, the world without and the world within; everything which, though it may indeed occasion the overthrow of faith and virtue in the conflict, thus puts them to the test, and may therefore serve also to confirm and strengthen them. In this more general sense it might, in itself considered, be understood here. But it is evident from the connection that here, as in many other passages, are meant the sufferings by which the Christian life is tried. Now to those who sigh under sufferings such as we have described, he addresses not merely the exhortation, to bear them patiently in the prospect of future glory. Far more than this. The feeling of suffering should lose itself in joy. They should do nothing but rejoice. How could James say this? It was because with him all has reference to what is noblest in man, what constitutes his true being, the imperishable, the inner man as it is termed by Paul. And knowing that these temptations, rightly used, must serve for the improvement of the inner man, and for this purpose were ordained of God; he therefore calls upon Christians not to be disquieted, but to rejoice in these sufferings, bearing in mind the end which they must promote for the children of God. The right improvement of suffering, on Christian grounds, is therefore presupposed, as indicated by James in the succeeding words: "Knowing that the trial of your faith worketh patience." It is here implied, that faith has its appointed process of development and purification in this life,—a process consisting in an unceasing conflict. Faith is in his view something **radically** different from, and elevated above, every other governing principle in man; something endued with an inward divine power; which must, however, approve itself in conflict with this opposing power, with all which proceeds from the flesh, from the natural man. There are indeed manifold trials of faith, and to all these the words of James apply. But it is the conflict with external circumstances, which is here especially meant. Here then is it to be tested, whether the faith is genuine, deep-rooted in the inner life; such an one as, through indwelling divine power, is able to overcome the world. The opposite case is presented by Christ, in what he says of the stony ground; where indeed the seed of the word springs up quickly, but soon withers because it has no sap (Luke viii. 6); a conviction which is not a firm and deeply rooted one, and in time of temptation vanishes away (v. 13). But so long as faith approves itself in this warfare, holds out in the conflict with the world, it demonstrates thereby its divine power. The test becomes an attestation. From the victorious contest faith comes forth with a confirmed constancy, and constancy manifests itself as a fruit of faith. It is by this means that the Christian first learns what he himself possesses.

But James well understood the character of the churches whom he addressed; and that among them the idea of faith was liable to the perversion of which we have spoken. It is everywhere his aim to counteract this one-sided tendency to the particular and the external. Hence he adds, that even if faith had thus approved itself as steadfast, in these outward conflicts with the world, yet this one thing alone would not constitute the Christian life. In manifold directions, must faith pervade the entire life, and manifest its power. "Let steadfastness," he adds (or as Luther translates it, patience), "have its perfect work." Luther understood this of time; it was to approve itself as perfect by persevering even to the end. But from the connection with what follows, and from the whole connection and course of thought in the Epistle, we should rather understand it thus: To the faith which has approved itself as steadfast, must correspond all the works pertaining to faith, the entire sum of the acts in which faith expresses its inward character. But James, in reference to the unity of the whole Christian life, designates the entire Christian course, all Christian action, as one perfect work,—as must be the case in order to

[Ch. i. 4, 5.]

correspond to true faith. Thus we can rightly understand what he immediately adds: "that ye may be perfect and entire, wanting nothing;" implying that with persevering faith connects itself the whole sum of the true Christian walk. By completeness is not meant an absolute perfection, nowhere to be found in the Christian life on earth; but, as often elsewhere in the Scriptures, all which belongs to Christian maturity, to what Paul terms Christian manhood,—as by wholeness ("entire") is meant the exclusion of whatever would mar the Christian life. When he desires that they may be wanting in nothing, he has in mind the aggregate of all qualities, powers, and capacities which Christianity develops, when its efficacy is fully proved as a leaven for the entire nature of man. Hence he subjoins a direction, intended to encourage them under the consciousness of any deficiency in this respect. He shows them what they must themselves do, if they would attain to that also, in which they are still deficient. What he might have expressed in wholly general terms, applicable to everything in which they might be conscious of deficiency, he applies (with his usual preference for the specific over the general idea) to that point especially wherein these particular churches might feel, or ought to feel, their need. Above all things was needed true wisdom, to give to the whole life its proper reference to the kingdom of God. Wisdom, or prudence (for which in the original the same word is used,—the prudence grounded in wisdom and subservient to it, the prudence of wisdom, of Christian love, being alone regarded as genuine) is by our Lord himself often held up as the chief object of attainment. But, as already remarked, there prevailed in these churches, as a fruit of the Jewish spirit, a proneness to a vain show of wisdom, to the over-estimation of mere knowledge, the conceit of knowledge and wisdom. So much the more did they need to be admonished, that true wisdom is based upon humility; that it is not to be learned in the schools from Doctors of the Law; that it can be obtained only from the fountain of eternal light. Hence James adds to what he has already said, "If any of you lack wisdom, let him ask of God, that giveth to all men liberally [with simplicity], and upbraideth not: and it shall be given him." Thus he counsels them, when they feel the consciousness of their deficiencies, to turn to God in prayer. God is designated as he who gives with simplicity, i. e. out of pure love, for the mere sake of giving,—simplicity being here contrasted with a liberality apportioned and limited by self-interest. He is represented as he who reproaches no one with his benefits, but who is ever ready still to give, if there only exists a susceptibility for his gifts. They should not turn then to such teachers as hold back from them a part of the truth, impart to them grudgingly, and reproach them with their indebtedness; but to the love of a Heavenly Father, who gives without measure and is ever ready to give.

It is prayer, therefore, which James represents as the condition required of the believer, in order that he may share in the communication from that heavenly fountain. This is the necessary relation between imparting and receiving in divine things. God alone being the Creator and Bestower, the human spirit can here only hold the attitude of a recipient. And this direction of the spirit, in order to receive what God is ready to impart, consists in prayer. The direction of the soul towards God in the feeling of personal need, and in the conviction that God alone can and will satisfy it, the longing towards God of the spirit hungering and thirsting after wisdom,—this is prayer. To seek the truth from God, and to pray, are one and the same thing. The whole life of the spirit, filled with this longing and impelled by it towards God, is prayer. So in those words of Christ,—to seek, to knock, in order to find the hid treasure, and to pray, are all classed together: "Ask and it shall be given you, seek and ye shall find, knock and it shall be opened unto you." (Matt. vii. 7.)

But in addressing churches so ensnared by tendencies to the outward in religion, it was all the more necessary to warn them against this in respect to prayer; which only then deserves the name, when it is the voice of the spirit itself, breathed from its inmost depths; lest they should suppose prayer in words, without that direction of the soul to God, to be all that was required. This warning is contained in the following words: "But let him ask in faith, nothing wavering." Trust in God is here represented as that direction of the spirit, from which prayer must proceed. To the eye of faith God must be present, as He to whom the prayer is directed. There must be the assurance, that he can and will supply the wants uttered before him, in order that it may be true prayer, prayer of the heart and not merely of the lips. The reason is immediately added, why prayer of the opposite character will not be heard. "For he that wavereth is like a wave of the sea, driven with the wind and tossed." Thus the steadfast direction of the soul to God is essential to prayer. But where there is doubt, there this ruling bias of the soul towards God is wanting. When, on the one side, the soul feels itself drawn towards God, and trust in Him begins to awaken; then on the other, the worldly tendency asserts itself, and strives to check the budding emotions of faith and trust. Hence the man, who is drawn hither and thither by conflicting inclinations, is compared to the wave, driven to and fro by storm and flood. James represents such a man as one who is at variance with himself, one in whom there exist, as it were, two souls;* who is unstable in all his ways, fickle-minded, unreliable in all his actions. Such is the character of his whole life, and his prayer answers to his life. In this it is implied, therefore, that prayer must be in consonance with the steadfast direction of the whole

* Eng. version, double-minded.—Tr.

life towards God; all must originate in one and the same temper of heart.

But here the question may be asked: How is this faith which is essential to prayer, to be obtained? Is one to abstain from prayer, because he lacks this measure of faith? But as in the words of our Lord above quoted, it is the necessary condition on which every gift of God is bestowed, that we knock, that we seek, that we ask of God; most surely faith is to be included, which is the gift of God, and always represented as something divinely wrought in man. He who is conscious of his lack of faith, who desires to believe more, to become stronger in faith, must in this also seek of God that wherein he is wanting. As that unhappy father in the Gospel narrative, of whom believing confidence was required in order to the healing of his son, cried out under a sense of the weakness of his faith, "Lord, help my unbelief!"; so will the feeling of that want of which we are speaking, of that lack of faith which stands opposed to true prayer, itself impel to prayer for strength to believe. He who is assaulted by doubts will turn his back upon doubt,—upon the world which threatens to ensnare his soul in unbelief, and will look to God; turning away from doubt, he will give himself to prayer. Thus through prayer will faith increase, and the strengthened faith will in its turn lend new power, new wings to prayer.

Thus have we seen how James, beginning with the exhortation to steadfastness under sufferings, was led on from one suggestion to another. [Ch. i. 9-11. Turning now his thoughts to the poor, who constituted a majority of these Christians, and who had much to suffer from the oppression of the rich, he addresses to them the consoling words: "Let the brother of low degree rejoice [glory] in that he is exalted." Instead of being cast down by the sense of his poverty, his low estate in respect to earthly relations, the Christian should rather feel himself raised above them, by the consciousness of an exaltation transcending all height of worldly honor; of that divine exaltation which is founded in the divine life, in the dignity of the Sons of God. This glorying he enjoins, with no occasion to apprehend self-exaltation; for the glory here spoken of is not one which man owes to his own powers and efforts; it is a dignity bestowed on him by God alone. This glorying is, therefore, the very opposite of all pride and self-exaltation, and can exist only in connection with true humility. But as this dignity is not adjudged to the poor on account of their poverty, so are the rich by no means excluded from it by their riches; although as we have already shown, these may to many become a hindrance in the way of their attaining it. To the rich, too, the way is pointed out, by which they may attain to that high dignity. "Let the rich," says James, "glory in that he is made low." That is: by humbling himself on account of that which passes with the world as great, he attains to the consciousness of that true dignity, which springs only from a sense of the nothingness of all earthly greatness. By this conviction of the worthlessness of his earthly riches, he is prepared to appropriate as his own the true riches, the only true dignity. Self-abasement is the path to true exaltation. So long as the rich man prides himself upon his wealth, and fancies that therein he possesses the true riches, the feeling of necessity for heavenly possessions, for true greatness, will not germinate in his heart. This very feeling of need, this desire, is the necessary condition of personal participation. Thus poor and rich among Christian brethren, must be united to each other by the same consciousness of equal dignity. James then goes on to picture the vanity of riches, by images drawn from the natural scenery of the East. Like the fresh grass, which at morning stands in all its flowery splendor, but under the scorching breath of the south wind suddenly withers and dies, so will the rich man perish in his ways. As he has his treasure only in earthly things, and has wholly merged himself in them, to him is transferred what is said of the vanity of those possessions, which he has made his all.

But the sufferings of the oppressed Christians are ever before the mind of James. Having spoken of these sufferings as trials for [Ch. i. 12-15. the verifying of their faith, he now extols as happy the righteous who endures temptation; since, by thus approving himself, he would win the victor's crown of eternal life, which the Lord has promised to all who love him. But how shall we reconcile with this the warning, not to ascribe temptations to God, which James immediately adds? Does he not regard God, as having himself ordained these sufferings as a means of testing faith? But there are different applications of this term, and we must distinguish between outward and inward temptation. The difficulties which beset one from without, may serve to awaken in him the latent power of the higher life. But they may also show his inward weakness,—may become the point of connection for that which stands opposed to the divine life. That which might otherwise have been the means of attesting his faith or Christian virtue, through his own fault becomes temptation to unbelief or to sin. Thus the outward temptation becomes an inward one, and thereby endangers the soul. When Christ bids us pray: Lead us not into temptation, this can certainly be no other than inward temptation; for his disciples were to be left behind, in the midst of those temptations of the world which should serve as tests of their faith. The object of the petition must have been, that the outward might not become an inward temptation. In like manner, James, in his use of the word, passes from one of these related ideas to the other.

But he must have found special reason for this warning in the peculiar state of these churches; and the explanation is to be sought in that same spirit of externalizing, of which we have already spoken. As this spirit shows itself in the conception of what is good, so does it also in the conception of sin. At no time have there been wanting grounds of excuse for sin; which men have regarded as something cleaving to them from without, and have sought its origin in merely external causes, instead of tracing it to its inward source in the faulty direction of the will. So it would seem that many in these churches excused themselves, on the plea that they were in subjection to a higher power, which hurried them away into sin. The Almighty, whom no one is able to withstand, has plunged them into these temptations. To this James replies: "Let no man say when he is tempted, I am tempted of God;" for as God cannot be tempted by aught that is evil, being elevated above all evil, so neither from him can temptation to sin proceed. The Holy One can tempt none to sin. He then lays open the fountain of temptation in man's own bosom, and describes the process by which the sinful tendency gains ground in progressive steps, till its final development in outward act. The source of temptation, he represents as lying in those desires inherent in every man, by which he is excited and led away; which lie in wait for him, as it were, but which he has power to withstand.

They gain strength only because they are not resisted; because he who might subject them to himself, submits himself to them. Thus prevailing, thus ripened into fruit, lust bringeth forth sin; and sin completed in act is followed by death.

We are by no means to infer, as is clear from the connection of thought in this passage, that these desires are not in their own nature sinful; or that the prevailing sinful tendency of the will would not involve death, even if it should find no expression in outward act, as though all turned on the outward act alone. The thought is this: Evil, from the first breaking forth of desire, proceeds on in ascending stages of development, until,—overpowering all the opposing influences of the higher life,—it is consummated in act. In this consummation in act is shown an increased strength of sin; and though man was previously able, by overcoming the enticements to sin, to maintain and to reestablish in himself the true life; yet now, through sin which has gained the victory over him, he falls a prey to death. James, therefore, warns them against indulging in such false and delusive ideas, as that God can be the author of evil.

Having thus directed them to look for the source

of temptation in themselves alone, and warned them against supposing that temptations could come from God; he now further [Ch. i. 16, 17. opposes to this delusion the thought,—that only whatever is good, whatever is true, proceeds from Him. As he is the Father of all material light, so is he also the Father of all spiritual light. With him, therefore, can be no alternation of light and darkness. From him, the unchangeable fountain of light raised above all darkness, nothing which tempts to evil can proceed. As light and all that is good, so darkness and all that is evil, are uniformly classed together in the Holy Scriptures.

From this general thought, James now passes again to its application to himself and his readers. To God alone were they indebted [Ch. i. 18. also for the dawning of the divine light on them, and for the new life thereby imparted. "Of his own will begat he us, with the word of truth, that we should be a kind of first fruits of his creatures." We here perceive in James, as in Paul, the opposite of the Jewish tendency to the outward. He presupposes in the Christian a moral transformation, wrought from within. The word of truth, the divine power of the Gospel, is that whereby the new higher life has been produced. He too describes this as something not consequent upon any human desert; all are indebted for it to the will of Him from whom all good proceeds. He too characterizes this moral transformation as a new creation. Those in whom it was first effected, he describes as the first-born of this creation; since from them it should continue to spread, till its final completion in a world pervaded and transformed by the divine principle of life.

But it is ever the manner of James to pass at once from the general to the particular; a trait originating partly in his own personal character, partly from the peculiar practical necessities of those to whom he was writing. He knew their disposition to content themselves with the general thought, without making an application of it to their own life. To incite them to this was his constant aim. He therefore proceeds at once to show how the divine word, received into the soul as the generative principle of the new creation, must manifest itself in the course of life. Neither does this take the form of a mere generality in his mind; but he passes directly to the special application most opposed to the practical errors of

[Ch. i. 19-21.]

these churches. We have already remarked on the propensity among them to assume the office of teacher,—the inclination to talk much and to do little; how they were thus led to pass judgment lightly upon others, to revile them, and how every passion found herein its nourishment. Against this he warns them in the words: "Wherefore, my beloved brethren, let every man be swift to hear, slow to speak, slow to wrath." One extreme must be driven out by the other. There is a self-willed silence, and there is a self-willed forwardness to speak. He who is inclined to be too inert and passive, to hold his peace when he ought to speak out boldly, must be exhorted not to give himself thus wholly to silence, but to be willing to speak when duty requires. But James is dealing with those, among whom the very opposite fault prevailed; those who lacked the sobriety, patience, and humility, to hear before they spoke; and of course he must make use of the opposite exhortation. As a warning against the temptation to anger, easily furnished by over-hasty speaking, he tells them that passion is least of all adapted to effect the work of piety. "For the wrath of man worketh not the righteousness of God." From the particular instance he now returns to the general thought with which he started, placing the two in close connection with each other. As passion forces man towards the outward, withdrawing him from the calm, ever-deepening inner life of the spirit, and banishing again from the heart that generative principle of the new creation, the Word of God, instead of allowing it to penetrate more and more the inner spiritual nature: he therefore counsels them to purify themselves from all that is evil, all excrescences of the inward life which passion nourishes, and in meekness to suffer the word implanted in their hearts to take deeper and deeper root therein. So shall they attain to the salvation of the soul, through the power of this word thus penetrating more and more their entire life. "Wherefore" (namely, because anger is in contrariety to the divine righteousness, and is the rank soil of every evil thing)—"lay apart all filthiness and superfluity of naughtiness, and receive with meekness the engrafted word which is able to save your souls." James, it is true, is addressing those in whom the ground of salvation was already laid; but he presupposes also, that they can only become partakers of salvation, by continuing to build on that foundation, and to yield submission to the word which they have once received, that they may experience in themselves its purifying and transforming power.

Having constantly in mind the practical errors under which these churches were suffering, he comes back again and again to the [Ch. i. 22-24. warning against that delusive tendency to exalt the outward. He exhorts them, not to imagine that it is sufficient to have a mere knowledge of the word, to be intellectually conversant with it. He warns them against the self-deception, that by such a knowledge merely they had complied with what he has just said, had really received the word into their life, had thus become Christians. The essential point is, the practical application of the word to the life. Herein must it manifest its efficacy, as a principle which works from within upon the outward character, and takes possession of the entire life. He says to them: "But be ye doers of the word and not hearers only, deceiving your own selves." He sets this in a clear light by a familiar illustration. He compares him who receives the word with the understanding only, without applying it to the life, to one who, having seen his image in a mirror, goes away and immediately forgets how he looked. Thus he who merely busies himself in a superficial way with the divine word, may have learned indeed what is the true aspect of his life in relation to the divine Law and its demands. A light has dawned upon his mind, as to what he is and should be. But turning away again from the divine word, hurried along by the current of life and by his own passions, he immediately forgets it all like him who just saw his image in the mirror, and all is of no avail. "For if any one be a hearer of the word and not a doer, he is like unto a man beholding his natural face in a glass; for he beholdeth himself, and goeth his way, and straightway forgetteth what manner of man he was."

With him who thus contents himself with a mere superficial study of the word of God, in whom knowledge and practice are at variance with each other, James now contrasts one who has looked into the depths of the divine Law, and lives in that contemplation. He here marks the distinction between the law of the letter, in its nature external, and that which Christianity has made the inner law, the law of the spirit, received

[Ch. i. 25.]

into the inner life. This he calls the perfect law, in contrast with the law of Moses viewed only in its externality, which as such,—that is, as a law of the letter merely,—can bring nothing to perfection, but leaves everything as it found it. The former he calls the law of liberty, inasmuch as it makes him free who has received it into his inner life, in contrast with the bondage of the letter. To this law one cannot hold the relation of a mere external hearer. Whoever has actually received it into himself as the perfect law, the law of liberty, is constrained by an inward impulse to manifest it in the outward life. " But whoso looketh into the perfect law of liberty, and continueth therein, he being not a forgetful hearer, but a doer of the word, this man,"—he adds,—" shall be blessed in his deed."

But how does this accord with Paul's representation, of the characteristic difference between the relations established by the Law and the Gospel, when he gives as the watchword of the former, " Do this and thou shalt live" (who does it, he shall live therein); and of the latter, " The just shall live by faith ?" There would indeed be a contradiction here, if James were speaking of the Law in the same sense as Paul,—if he meant that by works of law one could merit salvation. But this is far from James' purpose. He is speaking of the Law, as made by faith in Christ a living inward principle; of that Law as Christ unfolds it in the Sermon on the Mount, and which presupposes and includes in itself faith. In this view he may justly say, that one must feel himself blessed in the practice of this Law, and in this way alone can become a partaker of that blessedness which Christ imparts to the believer. It is precisely the same thing as Christ himself says, at the close of the Sermon on the Mount: "Whosoever heareth these sayings of mine and doeth them, I will liken him unto a wise man, which built his house upon a rock." Certainly, to this Paul also would have assented. To this certainly corresponded his own manner of teaching,—that only he can experience in himself the divine power of faith, can be blessed through faith, who furnishes the evidence of it in his life; faith being in his view that inward principle, which works from within the transformation of the whole life, that faith which works by love; as he himself says: "Though I had all faith, so that I could remove

mountains, and have not charity, I am nothing."
(1 Cor. xiii. 2.)

James now passes once more from the general to the particular, to the special application of what he has just said on this principle [Ch. i. 26, 27. of active obedience. The case which he presents, as requiring special notice, is selected with a view to the peculiar circumstances and faults of these churches. Writing to other churches he might have selected other examples. " If any man among you seem to be religious, and bridleth not his tongue, but deceiveth his own heart, this man's religion is vain." James takes for his starting-point the Christian principle, that religion must embrace the whole life. Hence he calls that religion merely imaginary, seeming, unreal, which allows the continuance of the moral defects originally predominant in the character; as, for example, in the application to these churches, that tendency to passionate anger, that want of control over the tongue. Of those who continued to live on thus as before, and yet made pretensions to religion, James says that they deceived themselves, that their religion was vain. Here again, in contrasting with this that religion which is genuine, showing itself in the life, he adduces the particular acts in which such a religion must manifest itself; in this, too, making the selection with special reference to the circumstances of these churches. To take the part of the orphan and the widow, to protect them against the pride and oppression of the rich,—this is pure and genuine religion. "Pure religion and undefiled before God and the Father, is this, to visit the fatherless and widows in their affliction, and to keep themselves unspotted from the world." He thus closes again with the general; the injunction, to keep one's self pure from all defilement by the world, having reference to the whole Christian life. He does not mean that external, often falsely conceived opposition to the world, which would hinder the Christian from serving as the true salt and the true leaven for the world. This would stand in direct contradiction with that course of active labors in the world, which James everywhere enjoins in this Epistle He means that one should keep himself inwardly unspotted from the world; that while externally acting upon it, he should guard himself against the infection of its impurity; that he should remain superior to the world, pure from the world whilst acting upon it. There are two things, therefore, essential to true religion and inseparable in it: viz. conflict against the evil which is in the world, the practical exercise of love; and in connection therewith, the keeping oneself inwardly pure from all ungodliness that reigns in the world. The former, moreover, cannot truly subsist except in connection with the latter.

We have already spoken of the distinction between the large numbers of the poor, and the much smaller number of the rich, in [Ch. ii. 1. these churches. Diversities and inequalities of condition, originating in the natural organization and relations of society, were not to be done away by Christianity, but rendered less grievous; were to be equalized by the common bond of love, and made a ground for the exercise of this Christian love. If it be true, (a matter on which we cannot decide with certainty) that the first glow of Christian enthusiasm gave rise for the time to a proper community of goods; yet was this a state of things adapted only to that period, when the new feeling of fellowship with each other in the divine life burst forth with a power, which for a while swallowed up all individual distinctions. But this could not be permanent. The inequalities founded in nature must at length re-appear, and the individual and personal be again allowed its just claims. Only the feeling should still remain, which united all as one heart and one soul; and through the love that cared for the wants of all, made as it were a common stock of the possessions of all. But this was now wanting in these churches; and the differences of rank and wealth were no longer repressed by the consciousness of that higher Christian equality. Hence, in opposition to such an unchristian aristocracy, James says: "My brethren, have not the faith of our Lord Jesus Christ the Lord of Glory, with respect of persons." He thus expresses the contradiction, between the disposition to estimate the worth of believers by such temporal advantages, and faith in Jesus as the Lord of Glory! To him who acknowledges Jesus as such, the one dignity of belonging to him must seem so great, that all personal advantages of an earthly nature must be less than nothing in comparison. His glory, in which all believers are called to participate, far outshines all earthly splendor.

He then proceeds with a more specific application

of this reproof. "For if there come unto your assembly a man with a gold ring, in goodly apparel, and there come in also a poor man, [Ch. ii. 2–4. in vile raiment: and ye have respect to him that weareth the gay clothing, and say unto him, Sit thou here in a good place; and say to the poor, Stand thou there, or sit here under my footstool: are ye not then partial in yourselves [at strife with yourselves], and are become judges of evil thoughts?"* The Greek word which we have translated "at strife with yourselves," indicates a state in which solicitude, doubt, conflicting thoughts, arise in the soul; as is the case where the simplicity of faith is disturbed, and discordant aims, worldly thoughts, take precedence of that one sole interest which should be all in all to the Christian. Here then are meant, in contrast with the Christian view of the equality of all who stand related in Christian fellowship, those worldly and foreign views, which give an undeserved deference to one, while they deny to another the respect due him as a member of the same community. These are the evil thoughts of which he speaks.

He now goes on to show them, from the history

* Those who judge from, or under the influence of, evil thoughts.—Tr.

of the spread of Christianity at this very time, from
the living example of the present, how
entirely such a way of judging is opposed
to the Christian stand-point. He appeals to the fact,
that on the poor pre-eminently have been bestowed
the highest dignity of the Christian calling, the
greatest riches in faith, the heirship of the kingdom
of Heaven. And they despised the poor, whom
God had so highly exalted! "Hearken, my beloved brethren; Hath not God chosen the poor of
this world, rich in faith, and heirs of the kingdom
which he hath promised to them that love him?
But ye have despised the poor." We must here
remark once more, that when James here speaks
of the kingdom of God as promised to those that
love him,—this love of God, in his sense of the
words, is doubtless to be understood as connected
with faith. He means Christian love; which presupposes the revelation of the redeeming love of
God in Christ, and the consciousness of this love
received through the Holy Spirit.

In contrast with these poor, among whom the
calling of God pre-eminently found access, he places the rich who oppress the
Christians, who drag them before the judgment-

seat,—if not on account of their faith, yet for the sake of extortion,—who blaspheme that holy name by which Christians are called. "Do not rich men oppress you, and draw you before the judgment-seats? Do they not blaspheme that worthy name by which ye are called?" We suppose that by the rich here are meant, such of the rich as were opposers of Christianity. James makes use of the well-known fact, that while the poor more readily received the Gospel, the proudly rich showed themselves the violent enemies of Christians and of Christianity. It is possible, indeed, though this would be less suited to the intended contrast, that rich men who called themselves Christians are meant; who might be said to blaspheme the name of Christ, through the scandal which they brought upon it by their course of life.

He calls on them to consider, how entirely such a course is at variance with the essential principle of the divine life,—viz. with [Ch. ii. 8-13. Love. With him, too, Love is the fulfilling of the Law. "If ye fulfil the royal law, according to the Scriptures, Thou shalt love thy neighbor as thyself, ye do well. But if ye have respect to persons, ye commit sin, and are convinced of the Law as transgressors." But he was dealing with persons ensnared on all sides in the outward and formal; who, therefore, among the transgressions of the Law (which they could not comprehend in its full majesty and strictness) made a difference in degree, as measured by an external standard; and who, judging by such a standard, might suppose it easy to satisfy the claims of the Law. To them such a predominance of the egoistic, as was shown in that preference of the rich, and that contempt of the poor, seemed no very grievous sin. It was therefore necessary to admonish them that the Law, as an expression, in one indivisible whole, of the divine will the divine holiness, demands absolute obedience; that only by such an obedience can one be justified, and that in every single act of transgression the whole Law is broken. "For whosoever shall keep the whole Law, and yet offend in one point, he is guilty of all. For He that said, Do not commit adultery; said also, Do not kill. Now if thou commit no adultery, yet if thou kill, thou art become a transgressor of the Law." Accordingly in applying this principle, in the sense of James, to the special case here spoken of, we must say: He who, in this one thing, permits his conduct to be determined by that selfishness which is in conflict with the law of love, has thereby violated the whole Law. He has violated it in reference to its substance, as the expression of the divine will wherein all is of equal dignity; and in reference to the ruling motive of his conduct, Self in opposition to Love.

Does James then mean, that in judging of sinful agents and acts no differences in degree can be admitted? By no means. It is only necessary to distinguish here between the abstract and the concrete, according as the question respects the principle itself in the unqualified strictness of its demands, or the varying relations which human agency bears to it; inasmuch as, while all must acknowledge themselves guilty before the Law, there may be gradations in guilt, according as the higher nature of man has more or less asserted its own freedom and superiority, or as the disturbing element of self may still show its predominance. Certainly James could not intend to say that any one, even among Christians, wholly meets the demands of the Law. The higher his conception of the dignity of the Law, as already shown, and the stronger his opposition to the usual standard of merit as consisting in particular external acts and observances,—the less could such a view be attributed to him. What immediately follows is to the same effect. It is assumed that, however different may be the actions of men, all appear as guilty in the sight of the Law. But as Christ teaches us to pray: Forgive us our debts as we forgive our debtors; so does James exhort, that by exercising gentleness and mercy, in the consciousness of still remaining sin, we should show ourselves meet subjects of the divine compassion. Christians should speak and act with the continual sense of their need of divine mercy; then will meekness in speech and action be its spontaneous expression, and mercy triumph over strict justice. In this view, therefore, he calls the law by which the Christian is judged, a law of liberty. For he is no longer under the yoke of a law requiring absolute obedience, which none can render, as the condition of salvation; but is connected with a law which is fulfilled by the free obedience of love, not of fear,—in the consciousness of sins forgiven and confiding reliance on the mercy of God. "So speak ye and so do, as they that shall be judged by the law of liberty. For he shall have judgment without mercy, that hath showed no mercy, and mercy rejoiceth against judgment."

As James everywhere marks the distinction between appearance and reality; and opposes those tendencies which make appearance pass for reality; as he declares himself against dependence on mere knowledge of the law without a corresponding course of life, against a pretended piety which does not show itself in works of love; so, from the same point of view and with the same connection of ideas, does he condemn a faith which fails to show itself in corresponding good works. "What doth it profit, my brethren, though a man say he hath faith, and have not works? can faith save him?" It should be carefully noted, that James does not say; if one has faith,—but if he professes to have it. He speaks of a merely professed faith, not of that which is genuine. Of such a faith, which by its want of good works proves itself to be spurious, he declares that salvation is not to be attained by it. In the view of Paul also, good works are necessary fruits of true faith. One which professed to be such, and yet was wanting in these fruits, he would not have regarded as justifying

[Ch. ii. 14–19.

faith, indeed would not have allowed it the name of faith. The meaning of James is clear from the illustration which follows. Faith without works, he compares to that love which never manifests itself in deeds, and is shown only in professions. "If a brother or sister be naked, and destitute of daily food, and one of you say unto them, Depart in peace, be ye warmed and filled: notwithstanding ye give them not those things which are needful to the body: What doth it profit? Even so faith, if it hath not works, is dead being alone [is in itself dead].

When James says that faith without works is dead, he certainly could not mean that works, the mere outward and phenomenal, constitute the living element of faith, that through them it becomes a living faith. On the contrary, he presupposes that true faith has life in itself, has in itself the living principle from which alone works can proceed, and that in works it makes itself known. The want of works was to him a proof that life was wanting in that faith, and hence he calls it a dead faith. He introduces a third person, speaking from James' own point of view with him who professes to have faith without works, and proving to him that the one cannot exist without the other. "Yea, a man may say, Thou hast faith, and I have works: show me thy faith without thy works, and I will show thee my faith by my works." In this James proposes,—for it is he who says this in the person of another,—to one who boasts of his faith though he has no works, that he should make the trial of showing to him the existence of his faith without the aid of works. To James it would be easy, by his works to show the faith which animates him, and in the strength of which those works were performed. As a proof that such a faith without works is of no value, he adduces the faith of evil spirits. Faith in God, in its true sense, can only there exist where he is consciously recognized as the highest good, where the whole life has reference to him; that faith which includes in itself a living fellowship with God,—a practical, not merely intellectual faith. With evil spirits, on the contrary, the consciousness of dependence on the Almighty and Supreme forces itself upon them against their will. They would gladly throw off this dependence, but they have not the power. It is something merely passive, with which their own free inclination, the self-moved submission of the spirit, has nothing to do. It is not a faith of the heart, but merely of the intellect; presenting God as in opposition to the spirit striving to escape from him,—God the Almighty, only as an object of fear to the spirit estranged from him, and unwilling to acknowledge him. "Thou believest there is one God; thou doest well: the devils also believe, and tremble."

By the Jews Abraham was claimed, as the representative of the faith in one God in the midst of nations devoted to idolatry; [Ch. ii. 20–24.] and therein was placed (as by others indeed in his circumcision) his great significance. James therefore proceeds to show, that the significance of this faith did not consist in a passive belief of the understanding in one God. It was a devotion of the whole life to God. It proved its genuineness by works of self-denial; by his readiness, in love to God and reliance upon him, in confiding resignation to his will, to deny all natural feelings and make of the object dearest to himself an offering to God. He, therefore, who would follow Abraham in his faith and by that faith be justified before God, must also attest his faith by like works of self-denial. "But wilt thou know, O vain man, that faith without works is dead? Was not Abraham our father justified by works, when he had offered Isaac his son upon the altar?" Thus might he say, that faith and works must here have wrought together. How wrought together? For the justification of man before God? So that Abraham could not appear as one justified before Him, until after the works had been performed? Had James intended this, it must have been on the supposition, that God can know man only so far as he manifests himself in outward acts. He could not therefore have recognized him as the omniscient God, who looks into the heart, and discerns the inward feeling before it comes to light. Recognizing his omniscience, he must have known that to the eye of God, this faith, which afterwards showed itself in such works of self-denial, already appeared as genuine justifying faith. But speaking from the stand-point of human consciousness, taking into account only the outward manifestation, he might so express himself; viz. that faith and works wrought together for justification. So also when he says, that "by works was faith made perfect," he could not mean that works,—the mere outward phenomena of faith,—are that which perfects faith itself; but only that in them faith shows itself genuine and complete, the attestation of faith in the life and conduct. "Seest thou how faith wrought with his works, and by works was faith made perfect? And the Scripture was fulfilled which saith, Abraham believed God, and it was imputed unto him for righteousness; and he was called the friend of God." And in that sense he then says: "Ye see then, how that by works a man is justified, and not by faith only."

To the example of Abraham he now adds that of Rahab. Here, also, against the false Jewish position, that this heathen woman was justified on the ground of passive faith in the One God, he declares that this faith was required to approve itself in works, the fruits of an inward disposition, contemning for the honor of God all worldly considerations. "Likewise also, was not Rahab the harlot justified by works, when she received the messengers, and had sent them out another way?" He concludes the whole discussion with the words: "For as the body without the spirit is dead, so faith without works is dead also." In this comparison, faith without works answers to the dead body without the animating spirit. But

[Ch. ii. 25, 26.]

it is only because the point of comparison is not fully brought out. We cannot suppose him to mean, that works answer to the spirit; for the spirit is certainly the inward, animating principle. Works, would answer to the activity of the living body. He means then: the want of works is proof that the faith is a dead one, destitute of the vital principle, and is therefore to be compared to a body which is dead.

James then passes to another, and at first view apparently quite different topic. But upon nearer inspection, it is found to be closely connected with the foregoing. [Ch. iii. 1, 2. For the very same tendency which made a merit of merely knowing and talking of the Law, of an empty show of faith without a corresponding life; would also lead men to set themselves up as teachers of others, and to have much to say in the assemblies of the church, without the inward call to this work. "My brethren, be not many masters [be not many of you teachers]." As the ground of this warning, he refers to the increased responsibility which one draws upon himself, by assuming to be the teacher of others; "knowing that we shall receive the greater condemnation." The ground of the tendency in these churches, to make so light a matter of teaching, was that very want of self-examination and self-knowledge, which had so much to do with all the faults rebuked by James. Under the influence of that superficial moral judgment, which took into account only the outward and apparent, they could not rightly estimate the importance of words. It was not considered, that speaking itself was an act, and was to be judged by a moral standard; and that one may sin, not less by the immoral use of speech than by any other act. He bids them beware of this danger. He shows how hard it is, to observe the just measure, to exercise the proper self-control, in the use of speech; what injury may proceed from a single word; and by this he would admonish them, to be so much the more conscientious in taking upon themselves the office of speaking. He who considered well that responsibility and its danger, could not so lightly resolve upon assuming it. Accordingly he says: "If any man offend not in word, the same is a perfect man, and able also to bridle the whole body." That is: He who on all occasions, exercises self-control in the use of words, will also be able to exercise the same in all other respects.

He then proceeds to show, by many striking examples drawn from actual life, what power may reside in things seemingly trivial,—how much depends on the government of the tongue. [Ch. iii. 3-8. "Behold we put bits in the horses' mouths, that they may obey us, and we turn about their whole body. Behold also the ships, which though they be so great, and are driven of fierce winds, yet are they turned about with a very small helm, whithersoever the governor listeth. Even so the tongue is a little member, and boasteth great things. Behold how great a matter [forest] a little fire kindleth! And the tongue is a fire,"— (that is, as a spark can set a whole forest on fire, so may a word spoken by the tongue be the occasion of great mischief)—"a world of iniquity: so is the tongue amongst our members, that it defileth the whole body, and setteth on fire the course of nature [life], and it is set on fire of hell." By this is meant, that as the tongue is set on fire by the flames of hellish passion, so from the tongue does the fire spread over the whole course of life. He then shows how vain a thing is man's dominion over the natural world, if he, aspiring to rule the world, is himself through passion a slave of the world; what a reproach it is to man, claiming subjection from all animals, not to be able to bridle his own tongue. "For every kind of beasts, and of birds, and of serpents, and things in the sea, is tamed and hath been tamed of mankind. But the tongue can no man tame; it is an unruly evil, full of deadly poison."

The show of piety James opposes in all its forms. Such is that pious cant, in which, along with praise to God in words, are mingled a hateful censoriousness and bitter denunciation of men, in whom God's image is to be honored. James exposes the inherent inconsistency of such conduct, which to his view is mere hypocrisy. "Therewith bless we God, even the Father; and therewith curse we men, which are made after the similitude of God. Out of the same mouth proceedeth blessing and cursing. My brethren, these things ought not so to be. Doth a fountain send forth at the same place sweet water and bitter? Can the fig-tree, my brethren, bear olive berries, either a vine figs? So can no fountain both yield salt water and fresh." Thus does James express

[Ch. iii. 9–12.]

the ground-thought of this whole Epistle, viz. that all turns on the inward temper from which the whole life takes its direction; and nothing could be more remote from that tendency, opposed by him at all points, which confines its regard to the merely external, to single acts and empty show.

As James has contended against a false faith, unaccompanied by works,—so does he, in like manner, against that knowledge and [Ch. iii. 13. wisdom in divine things, which does not make itself known by a living activity in a corresponding course of life. He requires of all religious knowledge, that it approve itself, as a product of the divine life of the spirit, in a course of conduct proceeding from that inner life. "Who is a wise man, and endued with knowledge amongst you? Let him show out of a good conversation, &c." With this view, he gives special prominence to that which stood most opposed to the faults of these churches; contrasting with the unbridled passion of those who made such account of their knowledge, the spirit of meekness as being the mark of genuine wisdom and knowledge: "let him show... his works with meekness and wisdom."

"But if ye have bitter envying and strife in

your hearts, glory not, and lie not against the truth." It is the inward temper which, in his view, marks genuine knowledge also, genuine wisdom. This must derive its being from above, must be the product of the divine life, and through its divine impress must make itself known also in the outward life. The opposite proceeds from a principle of the natural man, not from that which is divine. For the Holy Scriptures often designate, under the name of the Flesh, everything evil, all which stands opposed to the Spirit of God, to the divine life. When the term is used in this general sense, it includes also the spiritual nature of man,—the reason, the soul, in so far as it has not been made subject to the Divine Spirit, but claims an independent being, to be something in its own right,—independently of God and aside from God, and hence in opposition to him. All this is comprehended in the idea of the Flesh, in that Biblical sense. It is by no means limited to what we call Flesh, sensuality in the narrower sense of the term. From Flesh, understood in this more general sense, is distinguished in biblical usage that which in the narrower sense is designated as natural,*—viz. the spiritual nature of man (the reason, the soul) as being unlike to God, and conformed to the world. Reason, however highly developed and cultivated, remains still within the bounds of the natural man. It is of this James speaks; and this with him is the same which actuates apostate spirits. "This wisdom descendeth not from above, but is earthly, sensual [natural], devilish. For where envying and strife is, there is confusion, and every evil work."

He then enters more fully into particulars, and describes the traits which characterize genuine wisdom. He does this with special reference indeed to the false conceit of wisdom among these churches, but yet in a manner practically useful for all times. As characteristic of the wisdom that comes from above, he names first, purity,—i. e. freedom from all worldly stain; then [Ch. iii. 17.

---

* This term is used here, as already familiar to the reader of the English Bible, the same word in the original being so translated in several passages, e. g. 1 Cor. ii. 14. The German word (*seelisch*, of the soul, psychical, pertaining to the higher rational nature of man) is used by Neander, as explained in the text, of the rational soul not under the influence of the Holy Spirit,—in other words, of the *natural* or unrenewed mind and affections. It is therefore the best expression of his meaning to the English reader, though not a translation of the German word, for which we have no representative suitable to be used here.—Tr.

love of peace,—the truly wise not being stubbornly attached to his own opinion and contentious in support of it; then, that it is gentle, is easily persuaded,—i. e. ready to listen to others, willing to be taught, to acknowledge what is wrong on its own part, and to adopt the better way. All this gives evidence of victory attained over the love of self. The wisdom which is from above he farther characterizes, as full of mercy and good fruits,— meaning that knowledge and action must go together. We have already explained, in connection with a previous passage,* what James means by being in conflict with oneself. This he now excludes from the idea of genuine wisdom. He demands an inward harmony of soul, the stability of conviction.; that the soul shall not be distracted by the discordant views, the mental conflicts of this state of unbelief. It is difficult to indicate his meaning in a single word. Candor, simplicity, perhaps comes nearest to the idea. Finally, true wisdom is without hypocrisy.

In what James has thus far said, his main object has been to oppose the contentious spirit of this conceit of wisdom. He now

[Ch. iii. 18.]

* Page 71.

brings the opposite trait more prominently forward, by asserting that it is only in peace, in unity, that every Christian interest can prosper. "And the fruit of righteousness is sown in peace, of them that make peace." "Fruit of righteousness" may, in biblical usage, be variously understood. It may denote either the blessing which righteousness brings with it,—fruit for life eternal; or the fruits of righteousness in the works which it produces. But though the words are true in both senses, the latter seems to be the one intended by James,—and his meaning is: the seeds of all that is truly good in action, proceeding from righteousness, can only prosper where there is peace, and with those whose conduct tends to peace. Where all is strife, nothing truly Christian can prosper.

This leads him to speak, in general, of the source of the many controversies in these churches. This he finds in those insa- [Ch. iv. 1, 2. tiable desires which allow no one to be at rest. "From whence come wars and fightings among you? Come they not hence, even of your lusts, that war in your members?" Like Paul, James here presupposes an inward conflict in man, the conflict between flesh and spirit. As the power of evil is by Paul termed the law in the members, because in the body is the outward manifestation of man, and there the dominion of sinful desire shows itself; so James, in like manner, speaks of the lusts that war in the members. In the case of the unrenewed, the power of the sinful desires is opposed only by the activity of man's higher spiritual nature, which is too weak, however, to gain the victory over the opposing force. This conflict, which leads to no decisive result, and leaves man in unreconciled disunion with himself, is described by Paul in the seventh chapter of his Epistle to the Romans. It is otherwise with the Christian, the regenerated man. In him also this conflict is continued, but with this difference,— that in him the higher spiritual nature has been strengthened through the divine life imparted to him, whereby he is enabled to overcome the opposing sinful desires. But he must maintain the conflict in order to gain the victory; otherwise, the evil principle gains upon him more and more, and may at length succeed in wholly extinguishing the higher life. James exhorts to the maintenance of this warfare, and gives warning of the danger which threatens him who intermits it, as was the case with many in these churches. For there were doubtless many here, as appears from the rebukes of James, who called themselves Christians, but were yet strangers to the new birth, and stood in just the same relation to these two opposite tendencies as those who still belonged wholly to the world. Hence James says to them: "Ye covet" (namely earthly goods which ye may use in the service of your lusts) "and have not; ye kill, and desire to have [ye hate and envy], and cannot obtain."

In the original of the above passage it is said, "Ye murder." Luther has translated it "Ye hate," not without reason so far as respects the meaning; for it is hardly possible that James should speak of murder, in the proper sense, as so prevalent. But James purposely, without doubt, selects the very strongest expressions, in order to designate with the utmost precision the nature of that evil, which, whatever may be the outward form of manifestation, is still the same. Thus murder stands as the climax in the expression of hate and envy. For in the very nature of hatred and envy lies the desire, to remove their object out of the way. The selfishness which here betrays itself, sees in the existence of that object an obstacle to its wishes, from which it would gladly be freed. Even if the overt act has not yet been committed, and the power of the higher tendency is still too great to allow it, yet does it lie in the very nature of the emotion; and the divine word reveals to us, in the concealed germ of the heart, the very same thing which afterward, when expressed in act, becomes an object of general abhorrence. Hence Christ declares in the Sermon on the Mount, in opposition to the mere external conception of the Mosaic Law, that whosoever is angry with his brother, is in danger of the judgment, i. e. of damnation. And the Apostle John says: "Whosoever hateth his brother is a murderer."

James now directs them, as he had done at the beginning of the Epistle, to the fountain of all good, whence alone they could obtain all that was wanting to them, the supply of all their necessities. The ground of their unceasing and fruitless efforts, only involving them in strife, through the collision of selfish interests, he finds in their disposition to do for themselves, that which they should seek from God alone in the

[Ch. iv. 2, 3.]

spirit of humble submission. To their neglect of prayer, which alone can procure a blessing on labor, he ascribes their vain endeavors and contentions. Such were not wanting indeed in these churches, as connected a certain habit of prayer with all the other external practices of religion, and proceeding from the same temper of heart. But such prayer he characterizes as one which could bring no fruit, because it was not the true prayer of the heart, and did not proceed from the right disposition of the soul towards God. It was merely the expression of earthly desire, seeking to make God subservient to itself; for they sought from Him only what they might use for the gratification of their lusts. "Ye fight and war, yet ye have not, because ye ask not. Ye ask and receive not, because ye ask amiss, that ye may consume it upon your lusts."

He returns continually to the radical evil, the want in the soul of the one determining ground-tone in the reference of the life [Ch. iv. 4, 5. to God; the direction of the whole spirit to the world, in connection with many external practices of religion. As in the Old Testament, the union of the people with God is represented under the image of a marriage, their apostasy from God under that of adultery; so James addresses them as adulterers, inasmuch as they claimed to be worshipers of God, and yet served only the world. He admonishes them that God requires the whole heart, that it cannot be divided between God and the world; that either love to God or love to the world must be the animating principle; that devotion to the world, as the aim of effort, a love of the world which seeks in the world its highest good, cannot exist without hostility towards God,— as the Lord himself says: Ye cannot serve God and Mammon. "Ye adulterers, and adulteresses, know ye not that the friendship of the world is enmity with God? Whosoever therefore will be a friend of the world, is the enemy of God." James reminds them in general of the declarations of the Holy Scripture, which everywhere testifies of the incompatibility of these two radical tendencies. "Or," says he to them, "suppose ye that the Scripture saith in vain, The Spirit that dwelleth in us lusteth to envy [is a jealous spirit]?" This spirit, he would say, can suffer no other to share with itself; where it would take up its abode, it excludes the love of the world.

"But,"—to the above warning he immediately subjoins the consolation,—"He giveth more grace;" more, to wit, than that already bestowed, provided only that the one radical condition is fulfilled, in the entire submission of the heart, in the humbly receptive spirit. He reminds them of the passage from the Proverbs: "God resisteth the proud, but giveth grace unto the humble." Even if those, to whom his Epistle was directed, were not chargeable with the pride of unbelief,—they were yet wanting in the ground-tone of humility, the abiding sense of dependence on God, the ever-present consciousness that they were nothing and could do nothing without God. This want betrayed itself in excessive reliance on earthly possessions and human means. The prevalence of a worldly spirit always originates in want of humility. For this reason James admonishes them, that God withholds his gifts and aid from the proud, since the necessary condition on the part of the creature for the reception of every communication on the part of God, is wanting to them. But where humility is found, there is a susceptibility for the communication of all divine grace. He says to those, who

[Ch. iv. 6–8.

pleaded in excuse for sin the irresistible temptations of Satan, or the withholding of divine grace, that it was their own fault if they thus fell. All depended on the direction of their own will. In order to resist the Evil One, who has power over no one except by his own consent, they needed but to humble themselves before God, to turn to Him in the consciousness of dependence. Thus will God impart himself to them, and thus will the Evil One be compelled to flee. "Submit yourselves therefore to God: resist the Devil and he will flee from you. Draw nigh unto God and he will draw nigh unto you."

The inward and the outward James comprehends as one. Purity of heart from all worldly stains, must show itself in purity of the outward conduct. This is expressed by James (who delights to embody truth in a specific form) as keeping the hand, the instrument of sin, pure from every sinful act; and purity of life, exhibited in the external walk, must lead back again to its source, inward purity of heart. "Cleanse your hands, ye sinners, and purify your hearts, ye double-minded" (divided between God and the world). The Greek term expresses the

[Ch. iv. 8–10.]

idea (which we have already explained*) of a man who has as it were two souls; to whom is wanting the true harmony of the inner life, which proceeds only from the all-controlling direction of the soul to God; of the man who is divided between opposite tendencies to God and to the world. Such a spiritual state is in direct contrariety with that sanctification of the heart, which James requires; it being the very ground of true sanctification, that but one soul should dwell in man, that in all things the single animating principle should be love to God. It was therefore necessary, first of all, to arouse those who were sunk in worldly pleasure to a sense of the vanity of such enjoyments, to the wretchedness of their condition. A godly sorrow must be awakened in them; the anguish of repentance as a ground of true joy,— the joy in God of those who are dead to the world and wholly devoted to Him. So Christ says in the Sermon on the Mount, with which we find so many points of harmony in this Epistle: Blessed are they that mourn, for they shall be comforted. "Be afflicted" (feel your wretchedness), "and mourn, and weep: let your laughter be turned to

* Page 51.

mourning, and your joy to heaviness. Humble yourselves in the sight of the Lord, and he shall lift you up."

Thus James comprehends all in self-abasement before God, as the condition of all true exaltation, which comes alone from God; as the Saviour has said: Whoso exalteth himself shall be abased, and he that humbleth himself shall be exalted. James here speaks of an inward act of the spirit, not of one which can become an object of outward perception; although this inward act must make itself known in the outward form of the whole life. Hence he says,—abasement before God, in the eye of God, as that which can take place only between the soul and God. Here too the relation is such as man can sustain to God alone, not to any created being. He who is conscious to himself of such a relation to God, for that very reason will be far from placing himself in a similar relation to any human being. As his whole life thus has its root in conscious dependence on God, he will thereby be secured from every form of bondage to man.

The want of humility showed itself in that proneness to judge censoriously of others. Here was a twofold expression of the want of humility, in reference to the Law. He who judges thus censoriously of others, is [Ch. iv. 11, 12. far from humbling himself before that holy law; from comparing his whole life therewith, and discovering how great is the chasm between his life and its demands.

Hence James says, that such an one makes himself the judge of the Law, the lawgiver, instead of applying the Law to himself and acting in accordance therewith. Such an one, he says, in speaking against his brother speaks against the Law, since he gives the lie to the Law that accuses him for judging another. Furthermore, such an one betrays the want of self-abasement before God,—inasmuch as he forgets how he himself, with him whom he accuses, stands in like dependence on the One sole Judge and Arbiter of happiness and misery. He sets himself in the place of the Supreme Judge, inasmuch as he presumes to anticipate his verdict. "Speak not evil one of another, brethren: he that speaketh evil of his brother, and judgeth his brother, speaketh evil of the law, and judgeth the law; but if thou judge the law, thou art not a doer of the law, but a judge. There is one lawgiver, who is able to save and to destroy; who art thou that judgest another?"

The pride of the worldly spirit, in contrast with the nature of genuine humility, was the starting-point with which James commenced, and from which he proceeded to reprove the various forms of evil in these churches. In like manner he now brings forward another specific case, connected however with the same radical tendency of which we have spoken. It was that false reliance upon the Human, which leads one to make calculations upon the future, without for a moment taking into account the insecurity of human life; to form prospective plans of earthly gain, as if one were entirely certain of the future. James thought it necessary to admonish those, who were thus absorbed in worldly pursuits, of the uncertainty of all human things; that every moment of life is dependent on the will of God and his providence. "Go to now ye that say, To-day or to-morrow we will go into such a city and continue there a year, and buy, and sell, and get gain: whereas ye know not what shall be on the morrow: for what is your life? It

[Ch. iv. 13-17.]

is even a vapor which appeareth for a little time and then vanisheth away. For that ye ought to say, if the Lord will, we shall live, and do this or that." It is plain that in saying this, James did not mean to insist, that such a condition should always be expressed in words. For such expressions might easily degenerate into a mere form; and the tendency of these churches was to turn everything into form. Here again James shows his preference of the specific over the general. Instead of the general truth, of the uncertainty and dependence of the whole earthly life, he uses language adapted to suggest this general thought by its application to a particular case. From the particular he now passes over again to the general, and assails that false worldly and self-reliance in its whole extent. "But now ye glory in your vain confidence; all such glorying is evil." In closing this admonition, he warns them, that it is not enough to have known the truth here expressed; it was necessary,—and herein they chiefly failed,—that the known truth should pervade the life and control the conduct. "To him that knoweth to do good, and doeth it not, to him it is sin."

James now addresses himself to the rich, wholly immersed in the spirit of the world.

Ch. v. 1-6.]

"Go to now, ye rich men, weep and howl for your miseries that shall come upon you. Your riches are corrupted and your garments moth-eaten: Your gold and silver is cankered, and the rust of them shall be a witness against you, and shall eat your flesh, [as ye have treasured up fire] for the last days." He speaks of riches under three specific forms, viz. in the garnered fruits of the field, in garments, and in gold and silver. All these, he would say, the rich heap up without profit. Their treasures in gold and silver, allowed through disuse to consume with rust, will witness against them to their condemnation; showing their guilt in suffering to perish unemployed, that which they should have used for the benefit of others. The rust eats into their own flesh, inasmuch as it is a token of their own perishableness and of the judgment that overhangs them; as they, instead of gathering durable riches, have treasured up for themselves the fire of God's wrath in treasures accumulated for a prey to rust. He then describes the oppressions inflicted by the rich (not necessarily such as belonged to Christian churches) on the pious poor in humble life. "Behold, the hire of the laborers which have reaped down your fields, which is of you kept back by fraud, crieth: and the cries of them which have reaped are entered into the ears of the Lord of Sabaoth. Ye have lived in pleasure on the earth and been wanton; ye have nourished your hearts as in [for] a day of slaughter." That is; as one pampers the beast destined for slaughter, so have ye, giving yourselves up to the service of your lusts, and revelling in careless unconcern, prepared yourselves for the judgment that is hastening on. "Ye have condemned and killed the just, and he doth not resist you:"—the pious sufferer's patient resignation to God's will, in contrast with the pride and presumption of the oppressor.

He then turns to the Christian brethren, who had so much to suffer from the rich and powerful: He exhorts them to bear [Ch. v. 7, 8. with patience every wrong, to wait submissively for the coming of the Lord, who will redeem his own from all evil, and will show himself the righteous judge of all. We must bear in mind, that the time of the Lord's coming was then looked for as already near at hand. It was natural, in the Apostolic age, so to regard it. Christ himself had not chosen to give any information respecting the time of his coming. Nay, he had expressly said, that the Father had reserved the decision to himself alone (Mark xiii. 32); that even the Son could determine nothing respecting it. But still, the longing desire of the Apostolic church was directed, with eager haste, to the appearing of the Lord. The whole Christian period seemed only as the transition-point to the eternal, and thus as something that must soon be passed. As the traveller, beholding from afar the object of all his wanderings, overlooks the windings of the intervening way, and believes himself already near his goal; so it seemed to them, as their eye was fixed on that consummation of the whole course of events on earth. It is from this point of view that James here speaks. "Be patient therefore, brethren, unto the coming of the Lord: behold the husbandman waiteth for the precious fruit of the earth, and hath long patience for it, until he receive the early and latter rain. Be ye also patient; stablish your hearts: for the coming of the Lord draweth nigh." James,—who, as already remarked, had all the oriental fondness for imagery drawn from natural objects,—here transfers to history the laws of gradual development in the phenomena of nature. As the fruits of the earth mature only by slow degrees, and the husbandman must wait patiently for the early and the latter rain; so there is needed the same constancy of patience, while anticipating the final consummation of earthly history, in its gradual course of development. Here, too, everything has its appointed time; and one must guard against that impatient haste, which is unwilling to wait for the successive stages of progress, and is eager to reach the end at once.

He now proceeds to speak of the deportment of Christians towards each other, and commends the mutual exercise of long-suffering and forbearance. [Ch. v. 9-11. They should not indulge in mutual accusations, appealing to God against one another, but leave all to the judgment of God. They should not desire, by thus mutually condemning one another, to anticipate the Judge who will soon appear. His words remind us of our Saviour's admonition in the Sermon on the Mount: Judge not, that ye be not judged. "Grudge not one against another, brethren, lest ye be condemned: behold the judge standeth before the door." He then sets before them the examples of the prophets as models of patience; especially the example of Job, in whom, after he had endured every trial of his patience, the mercy of God was so gloriously displayed. "Take, my brethren, the prophets, who have spoken in the name of the Lord, for an example of suffering affliction and of patience." The thought is doubtless this: They have spoken in the name of the Lord, and yet have suffered so much,—and that for the Lord's sake. If the prophets, so highly honored and speaking in the name of the Lord, have endured such suffering, how could we expect a different lot? "Behold we count them happy which endure. Ye have heard of the patience of Job, and have seen the end of the Lord" (i. e. the end brought about by him, the final issue which the Lord granted to all his trials); "that the Lord is very pitiful and of tender mercy."

Then follow particular admonitions and exhortations, all which, however, are opposed in spirit to such errors, as were the fruit of the leading evil tendencies in these churches. In the Sermon on the Mount, Christ has unfolded the

[Ch. v. 12.]

whole Law in its spirituality and glory; everywhere converting the outward and particular to the inward, to the completeness and unity of the inward temper and disposition; at once abolishing and fulfilling the Law, abolishing it in the letter and fulfilling it in its spirit. Thus to the command: Thou shalt hallow the seventh day, is given its higher spiritual import,—Let every day be holy to thee. In like manner, the requirement to regard an oath as holy, becomes in its true spirit: Let every word be holy to thee, as being consecrated to the Lord,—as addressed to him, since he is ever before thine eyes. What an oath is to others, shall every word be to the Christian. Hence among true Christians, there will be no need of oaths; since to each his word is holy, and such is the mutual confidence of all, that the word of each is so received among them. So should it be in a truly Christian church, in which all are recognized as genuine Christians. But in these churches, where the proneness to much speaking had naturally led to a careless use of words, there now prevailed the Jewish habit of using many asseverations, in order to give their words a weight which they had not in themselves.

Even if they shunned so frequent a use of the name Jehovah, they had other more covert forms of oath in its place,—the violation of which, however, they made less a matter of conscience. Against this James says expressly: "But above all things, my brethren, swear not; neither by Heaven, neither by the earth, neither by any other oath. But let your yea be yea, and your nay be nay; lest ye fall into condemnation." That is, their Yea and Nay should suffice in place of every other form of confirmation; for if their word is not in itself sufficient, and requires the aid of protestations to procure belief, they bring themselves into condemnation.

Then follows the general direction, which most of all stands opposed to the spirit of worldliness in these churches, to that tendency to distinguish between certain acts of religious worship and all the rest of life as belonging to the world. Nothing can be more opposed to such a tendency than the requirement, that every feeling of the Christian, in sorrow and in joy, shall take the form of prayer. Thereby are sorrow and joy to be sanctified and ennobled. In suffering, the feeling of pain shall be changed to

[Ch. v. 13.]

the tone of prayer; from God is help to be sought in prayer,—power to sustain suffering and to be submissive under it. And joy, too, shall attune the heart to the praise of God, to gratitude towards Him to whom we owe every good. Thus shall sorrow and joy have this in common,—the direction of the heart towards God. And as life is divided between joy and sorrow, the whole life will thus become prayer. "Is any among you afflicted, let him pray. Is any merry, let him sing psalms."

Having thus referred everything to prayer as the soul of the Christian life, he now makes a specific application of the principle to cases of sickness. [Ch. v. 14-18. Here there was need of mutual intercession in the name of the Lord. As the Presbyters acted in the name of the whole church, and each one as a member of the body felt that he needed its sympathy and intercession, and might count upon it; individuals should therefore, in cases of sickness, send for the Presbyters of the church. These were to offer prayer on their behalf. With this was connected a symbolical transaction,—practised indeed in many churches of the East, but never prescribed as a general usage,—the anointing with oil; of which Christ had sometimes made use in the healing of the sick, as an outward sign of healing and sanctifying power. If it was the will of the Lord, the sick should be restored to bodily health. But, however this might be, he should certainly receive spiritual refreshment, the renewed and strengthened consciousness of sin forgiven; and this could not but favorably affect his bodily state. "Is any sick among you? Let him call for the elders of the church, and let them pray over him, anointing him with oil in the name of the Lord; and the prayer of faith shall save the sick, and the Lord shall raise him up: and if he have committed sins, they shall be forgiven him." We see that James ascribes the healing power, not to the anointing with oil, but to the prayer of faith. As he regards the Presbyters in the light of organs of the church, acting in its name; so does he hold all other Christians in such a relation, as members of one body, that they should mutually pray for one another in bodily and spiritual need; should confess their sins to one another, and pray for the forgiveness of each other's sins. He ascribes great efficacy to the prayer of fraternal love. "Confess your faults one to another, and pray one for another, that ye may be healed,"—whether spiritual and bodily healing united is meant, as in the last quoted passage, or merely spiritual healing. "The effectual fervent prayer of the righteous man availeth much." Of this efficacy of prayer he adduces examples from the Old Testament. But the Jewish tendency to externalize everything, led them to contemplate these holy men of old only from a distance, and as objects of veneration and wonder, not as examples for imitation. James therefore reminds them, that these men were frail mortals like themselves, and that the power of God can still work through the weak. This application was all the more appropriate, inasmuch as Christianity, by virtue of the common relation of Priest and Prophet belonging to all believers, had made that common to all which under the old dispensation had been the gift and prerogative of a few. "Elias was man subject to like passions as we are, and he prayed earnestly that it might not rain: and it rained not on the earth by the space of three years and six months. And he prayed again, and the heaven gave rain, and the earth brought forth her fruit."

This exhortation to mutual intercession, in bodily and spiritual need, leads to this further admonition,—that they should not harshly spurn from them such as, in their religious and moral development, may have erred from the right way, but should interest themselves in their case and seek to lead them back to the truth: an admonition which they specially needed, who were so prone to defame and condemn. "Brethren, if any of you do err from the truth, and one convert him, let him know, that he which converteth the sinner from the error of his way, shall save a soul from death, and shall hide a multitude of sins." This, then, is in James' view the highest work of love,—to rescue the fallen brother from that spiritual death to which he is verging. More than to excite in one repentance for a single sin, and thereby prepare the way for attaining forgiveness of one sinful act,—more than this is the rescue of a soul from a life of sin, and the restoration of the new divine principle of life. By this the many sins are covered, in which his former course had plunged him. This explanation of the words seems most in harmony with the connection. But, by the sins here spoken of, might be understood the sins of him who thus rescues a brother from death. The meaning would then be: The love thus shown in active zeal for the spiritual welfare of another, shall cover many sins into which one may have fallen through infirmity of the flesh; inasmuch as Love outweighs all else, and above all else is adapted to subdue the still remaining evil of the heart. So we are taught by the Saviour himself, that to him who loveth much, much shall be forgiven. Were this the true meaning of the passage (which, however, is contrary to our view), still the covering of one's own sins would not be dependent on the success of his efforts for another; for this is not placed in the power of man, and he can gain nothing for himself thereby, for the very reason that it is something independent of his own purpose. It is the zeal of love, laboring for the conversion of another,—it is this that hides the multitude of sins!

Thus closes this Epistle, in that spirit of love which breathes through it all, and which everywhere shows itself in the life and labors of James!

www.ingramcontent.com/pod-product-compliance
Lightning Source LLC
Chambersburg PA
CBHW071142090426
42736CB00012B/2198